PREVENTING FRAUD
IN NONPROFIT
ORGANIZATIONS

PREVENTING FRAUD IN NONPROFIT ORGANIZATIONS

EDWARD J. McMILLAN, CPA, CAE

WILEY

John Wiley & Sons. Inc.

Copyright © 2006 by John Wiley & Sons, Inc., Hoboken, NJ. All rights reserved.

Published by John Wiley & Sons, Inc., Hoboken, New Jersey.
Published simultaneously in Canada.

Limit of Liability/Disclaimer of Warranty: While the publisher and author have used their best efforts in preparing this book, they make no representations or warranties with respect to the accuracy or completeness of the contents of this book and specifically disclaim any implied warranties of merchantability or fitness for a particular purpose. No warranty may be created or extended by sales representatives or written sales materials. The advice and strategies contained herein may not be suitable for your situation. You should consult with a professional where appropriate. Neither the publisher nor author shall be liable for any loss of profit or any other commercial damages, including but not limited to special, incidental, consequential, or other damages.

For general information on our other products and services, or technical support, please contact our Customer Care Department within the United States at 800-762-2974, outside the United States at 317-572-3993 or fax 317-572-4002.

Wiley also publishes its books in a variety of electronic formats. Some content that appears in print may not be available in electronic books.

For more information about Wiley products, visit our Web site at http://www.wiley.com.

Library of Congress Cataloging-in-Publication Data

McMillan, Edward J., 1949-
    Preventing fraud in nonprofit organizations / Edward J. McMillan.
        p. cm.
    Includes index.
    ISBN-13: 978-0-471-73343-0 (pbk.: alk. paper)
    ISBN-10: 0-471-73343-1 (pbk.: alk. paper)
        1. Fraud—Prevention. 2. Nonprofit organizations—Management. I. Title.
    HV6691.M36 2006
    658.4'73—dc22

                                                            2005046642

Printed in the United States of America

10 9 8 7 6 5 4 3 2 1

Contents

About the Author

Edward J. McMillan, CPA, CAE, is an experienced fraud examiner and teaches fraud prevention courses to organizations such as the American Institute of CPAs, the Maryland Association of CPAs, other state societies of CPAs, the U.S. Chamber of Commerce, and the American Bar Association, among others. Ed also speaks regularly on the subject of fraud prevention at business conventions of all types and can be reached at (410)893-2308 or contacted via email at emcmillan@sprintmail.com.

Acknowledgments

The publisher and author would like to extend gratitude to the following organizations for their generous permission to reprint their copyrighted materials in the body and glossary of this manual:

The American Chamber of Commerce Executives
Fraud and Embezzlement in Small Business:
How It Happens, How You Can Prevent It

Association of Certified Fraud Examiners
Glossary

Preface

Unfortunately, embezzlement and fraud are a reality that all organizations are confronted with.

This manual is designed to help auditing CPAs, internal auditors, fraud investigators, and management understand how to thoroughly evaluate the system of internal controls, expose weaknesses that could lead to fraud, and take corrective action to reduce the possibility of victimization.

Obviously this book cannot guarantee that fraud or embezzlement will be eliminated. However, if the suggestions offered in this manual are implemented, this risk will be reduced substantially.

Disclaimer

The contents of this book should not be construed as legal advice, and in that respect the publisher and author assume no liability or responsibility accordingly. Before implementation, the internal controls, policies, and forms suggested in this book should be reviewed by a competent attorney to ensure compliance with federal, state, and local laws.

Implementing the internal controls, forms, and processes in this book will by no means guarantee that an organization will be protected from fraud. While this book may help to decrease the *possibility* of embezzlement, it is imperative to remain diligent in business practices.

Remember, desperate people resort to desperate action, and where there is a will, there is a way.

About the Companion Website

The sample policies and procedures found in Section Six of this book are also available in MS-Word format on a Web site designed to accompany this book:

www.wiley.com/go/mcmillan_nonprofit_fraud

They can be copied and customized to fit the specific needs of your organization.

Editor's Note: The author has also written a similar book (Wiley 2006) on the subject of fraud prevention policies and procedures designed for the business community entitled:

Policies and Procedures to Prevent Fraud and Embezzlement: Guidance, Internal Controls, and Investigation

Not-For-Profit Organizations: Four Consistent Areas of High Risk Embezzlement: Who Does It and When

Not-For-Profit Specific Issues

WHEN AUDITING CPAs audit an organization, they are required to have a good understanding of the nature of their client's business to enable them to evaluate risk factors that could lead to embezzlement and to suggest corrective action accordingly. Obviously, business environments vary according to the nature of the business, because the risks banks face are substantially different from the risks an automobile dealership faces.

Although auditing CPAs, internal auditors, and management should continually strive to reduce embezzlement risks of the not-for-profit organization as a whole, history has shown that a typical nonprofit has extremely high fraud risk in four specific areas, those being:

1. Checks *mailed* to the organization's offices from members, advertisers, and the like

2. Printing expenses

3. Postage expenses

4. Personnel-related expenses including wages, payroll taxes, and employee fringe benefits

This book will address these areas in greater detail in later chapters, but because of the high likelihood that a knowledgeable person could take advantage of weak internal controls in these four areas, it is important to understand why these areas are so susceptible to fraud and why basic corrective action must be taken.

Checks Mailed to the Organization:

Issue: Not-for-profit organizations in general are unique in that they are *widely known by their acronyms* by both their members and the public! For example, the American Medical Association is referred to as AMA, the National Rifle Association is called NRA, and so forth. The vast majority of nonprofits are known by their acronyms.

Risk: When members, advertisers, and the like remit payments to non-profits, often the remittance check will be made payable simply to the organization's acronym rather than the full name of the entity.

What could an individual with access to checks do to perpetrate a fraud? Simply open an account in another bank using a clever variation of the legitimate organization's name, with the same acronym. For example, someone at the American Crayon Association (ACA), could open an account for the nonexistent Apple Collectors Association (another ACA) at another bank and easily divert checks payable to ACA to the second account.

Suggestion: 1. Utilize the bank's Lockbox Service whereby members and contributors are provided with remittance envelopes, and checks are mailed directly to and deposited by the organization's bank rather than mailed to the organization. This service effectively eliminates the risk associated with diverting checks made payable to an acronym because employees never come into contact with these checks.

Important—see "Lockbox" in Section 3 of this manual for an in-depth discussion of this service.

2. On invoices, dues billings, and the like, request checks be made to the full legal name of the organization rather than its acronym.

Printing Expenses:

Issue: In most not-for-profit organizations, the primary product is the printed word (magazines, newsletters, books, brochures, etc.) and printing expense is typically a substantial portion of the overall budget, and in that respect, susceptible to fraud.

Risk: Because printing is such a major portion of the budget, the organization must be vigilant in monitoring internal controls over printing, to avoid ghost printing vendors and collusion between printers and key staff.

Suggestion: Ensure the organization has thorough and continually updated Approved Vendor Files. These files should include detailed information such as legal entity name, remittance address, street address, contact name, federal identification number, emergency numbers, and so on. This information is vital to auditing CPAs and internal auditors when reviewing records.

Important—see "Ghosts on the Payroll and Ghost Vendors" in Section 4 of this manual for more in-depth discussion.

Postage Expenses:

Issue: As with printing expenses, not-for-profit organizations typically have a substantial budget for postage (and freight), because they would probably have, at a minimum:

- ➤ First class mail
- ➤ Business reply mail
- ➤ Bulk mail
- ➤ Media mail
- ➤ Second class mail
- ➤ Postal permits

Additionally, nonprofits often also do business with:

- ➤ Mail and fulfillment houses
- ➤ Commercial couriers such as UPS, FedEx, and the like

Once again, because of the high volume of mail that a typical not-for-profit experiences, the organization must be vigilant in ensuring that postage funds are not diverted.

It is a simple matter for knowledgeable persons to "sell" organization postage to another party, divert postage for their own use, prepare checks to nonexistent mail houses, open up accounts using clever variations of commercial couriers' acronyms or names, and so forth.

Suggestion: It is imperative that postage expense be monitored very closely and routinely by auditing CPAs, internal auditors, key staff, and others.

Important—see the "Postage Issues" and "Ghosts on the Payroll and Ghost Vendors" in Section 4 of this manual for in-depth discussions and recommendations.

Personnel Expenses:

Issue: Risks associated with personnel-related expenses are obviously not unique to nonprofits, and all businesses have a high risk in this area. Why? Typically upper management rarely is aware of the detail associated with processing payroll, calculating Social Security and Medicare, calculating federal and state income tax withholding, and other areas related to payroll.

When management is unaware of the detail associated with processing payroll, they are highly susceptible to payroll fraud.

Suggestion: 1. Always ensure that *two* employees are involved with processing payroll, and both employees sign the payroll detail attesting accuracy.

2. Consider direct deposit of employee pay. Direct deposit requires bank account numbers, creating an audit trail.

3. Have either the auditing CPA or internal auditor pay a surprise visit to the organization to check the accuracy of payroll, ensure there are no ghost employees, and so forth.

Important—refer to ghost employee and other personnel-related information in this handbook for greater in-depth discussion and recommendations.

Summary

Although there are obviously other areas of risk such as travel expenses and the like, it is clear that the four areas noted in this chapter are of paramount importance when evaluating the risk associated with a typical not-for-profit. Published operating ratio reports for nonprofits consistently report that if a nonprofit is victimized, there is a high likelihood that one of these areas is involved.

The Perpetrators: Who They Are, Why They Do It, and How They Are Caught

In the real world of embezzlement, the perpetrators rarely fit the stereotypical image of someone capable of concocting and carrying out fraud schemes. Rather, they are almost always someone *above suspicion!* The stories of internal theft being carried out by the innocent-appearing young man who sings in the choir or the older woman whom you can count on to remember everyone's birthday are actually the norm. Embezzlers are of any age, sex, race, religion, and income bracket.

Why? Despite the appearance of honesty, you can never be sure of what is going on in someone's personal life, and desperate people are capable of taking desperate action. For example, it is probable that you have no idea that a fellow employee may:

➤ Have a gambling issue
➤ Have an alcohol problem

➤ Have a substance abuse situation

➤ Be experiencing financial difficulties

➤ Have expensive medical bills

➤ Or—enjoy living life on the edge!

There are, however, a few profiles that warrant the attention of management:

Who They Are, Why They Do It

The Disgruntled Employee   Employees who have been passed over for promotion, demoted, reprimanded, or been the subject of disciplinary action often feel they have a justifiable grievance against the organization. People in this situation often feel they have nothing to lose if they are caught in wrongdoing. Additionally, they often rationalize their actions and feel they are justifiably righting a perceived wrong, and they convince themselves they have done nothing wrong.

The Stressed-Out Employee   People experiencing a personal crisis such as a divorce, serious illness, or death in the family often become desperate. It is worth repeating that desperate people often take desperate actions.

Employees Living above Their Means   Employees living an extravagant lifestyle well above their income level are always suspicious. Money needed to fund this lifestyle had to come from somewhere!

The Employee Who Never Takes a Vacation   It is unnatural and unhealthy for people never to take time off. Unfortunately, the reason for this behavior is often that they can't risk having someone else sit at their desk, look at their mail, or answer their telephone because they are hiding something.

Employees Who Are Unnaturally Compulsive about Their Job Responsibilities As in the case of the employee who never takes a vacation, employees who refuse to share their work with anyone, hide their work, or take work home could also be covering something.

Employees Experiencing Financial Difficulties   People who can't meet their debts and are stretched too thin financially are always of concern. When this situation comes up, consider helping the individual by providing personal financial counseling.

Unfortunately, people sometimes find themselves in dire circumstances. Often this occurs through no fault of their own. There may be health issues, financial difficulties, layoffs, or elderly parents needing assistance. Always remember that desperate people will take desperate action.

Note: Occasionally check where people cash their paychecks. A bank or credit union is the typical place. If an employee owes money, you may see an endorsement over to a private citizen. You may even see checks cashed at liquor stores, pool halls, bars, or other odd places. Or an employee may be using an expensive check-cashing service. Be alert. This may indicate an employee with problems. So a simple review of paycheck endorsements is imperative.

Employees Who Have Drug Problems   People who become addicted to drugs will do almost anything to support their habit, obviously including stealing from their employer. The best way to approach this is to suggest counseling. This type of person should never, of course, be put in a position handling money, checks, and so forth.

The Employee with a Gambling Problem   Most gamblers, of course, are responsible individuals, but people with a gambling problem, particularly illegal gambling through bookies, are a real danger. These people "borrow" money to place bets and intend to repay the "loan" with their winnings, which of course rarely happens. When these people get in over their heads, particularly with the criminal element, they find themselves in a desperate situation and, once again, desperate people will resort to desperate actions.

The Fraud Triangle

To preview the Fraud Triangle noted in "Statement of Auditing Standard No. 99", Section 2 of this handbook:

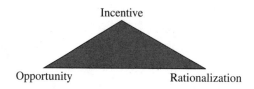

Incentive: The scenarios described above are examples of the "Incentive," the starting point for fraud.

Opportunity: Too much trust, poor internal controls, lack of supervision by supervisors, no financial audit by independent CPAs, and the like, all create opportunity for fraud. The basic purpose of effective internal controls is to remove the opportunity for fraud.

Rationalization: After a period of time, the perpetrator actually convinces himself that he is not stealing, but rather self-correcting a perceived wrong such as a pay discrepancy or the like.

How They Get Caught

Just as profiles of embezzlers surprise people, so does uncovering fraud.

Despite belief to the contrary, *most fraud is discovered by accident and due to unanticipated work interruptions,* and not during the course of a CPA's financial audit!

Here is how fraud is uncovered:

➤ During the course of a CPA's financial audit: 2%
➤ As the result of an internal audit: 18%
➤ By whistleblowers: 30%
➤ By pure luck: 50%

Let's break down each category:

CPA Financial Audit   Despite belief to the contrary, it is actually unusual for an audit to uncover an embezzlement. Why? The perpetrator knows what the auditor does and does not look at, as well as what management does and does not look at. This combination, coupled with a weakness in internal controls, is the basis for the important "opportunity" portion of the Fraud Triangle. It is also important to reinforce the fact that auditors are not there to uncover fraud during the course of their audit, but rather to issue an opinion on whether or not the figures in the financial statement are presented fairly, even considering the provisions of SAS 99.

Internal Audits   As you can see, the probability of uncovering fraud rises from just 2% due to a CPA's audit to 18% for an internal audit.

A good internal audit program is very effective if the procedures are followed during the period between the time that the auditors conclude field work for year 1 and return to start field work for year 2. See "The Embezzler's 'Window of Opportunity,'" later in this chapter.

Whistleblowers   The probability of fraud being detected rises to an impressive 30% due to whistleblowers.

It is important to have a whistleblower program coupled with a whistleblower retaliation prohibition policy as part of any organization's administrative policies. These policies are actually a requirement of organizations subject to the Sarbanes-Oxley Act of 2002, but all organizations should give this serious consideration. (See "Whistleblowers," in Section 3 of this handbook.)

Luck   Luck accounts for a whopping 50% of all reported fraud! That is correct—simply stumbling onto something or the thief's carelessness accounts for a full one-half of reported fraud!

The Finance Department

It's unfortunate, but it's a fact—*most* internal embezzlement schemes involve someone assigned to the accounting function. With that in mind, pay particular attention and be diligent when assessing a system of internal controls.

Think about some of the responsibilities individuals have in the typical accounting area:

➤ They receive the organization's checks and cash.
➤ They prepare the bank deposits.
➤ They take the deposits to the bank.
➤ They order checks.
➤ They prepare checks.
➤ They mail checks.
➤ They receive the bank statements.
➤ They prepare payroll.
➤ They prepare payroll tax deposits.
➤ They do the bank reconciliations.
➤ They prepare the financial statements.
➤ They prepare journal entries.
➤ They are the petty cash custodians.
➤ They prepare payroll tax returns.
➤ They have access to the safe.
➤ They activate loans and lines of credit.
➤ They are the sole custodians of the accounting records.
➤ They coordinate and arrange for payment for organization credit card transactions.
➤ They process credit card information from customers.
➤ They prepare W-2s and 1099s.
➤ They process credit card transactions for customers.
➤ They are the custodians of fixed asset records.
➤ They are the custodians of inventory records.
➤ They ultimately write off bad debts from accounts receivable.
➤ They record debt service transactions.
➤ They account for noncash expense such as depreciation and amortization.

Without effective internal controls, any of these responsibilities, in the hands of the wrong individual, could lead to a serious problem. This problem is compounded if the person the accountant reports to is not an accountant also.

When Do They Do It?   In addition to the fact that embezzlers are often above suspicion, many fraud schemes have another similarity. The time of the embezzlement is very likely the same from case to case.

And, exactly, when is that? It's always during a very large "window of opportunity." And that window is most likely to be open *between the time the CPA has left the office after concluding the audit field work for the current year, and the time he or she is scheduled to come back to start the audit for the subsequent year.*

The window of opportunity is the time that the organization has to be the most vigilant. A smart thief is not going to pursue an embezzlement scam when the auditors are on-site or due to come in. In fact, this is the time when the thief will be squeaky clean.

The Embezzler's "Window of Opportunity"

Any accountant experienced in the area of fraud investigation or forensic accounting will emphasize the vital importance of taking thorough and copious notes of every important detail relating to the investigation. Why? Notes will be extremely important in the event that the matter goes to litigation, because it may be *years* before the matter goes to trial. Obviously, people move on to other firms, people retire, and there is an understandable memory lapse over time. If good notes are taken, others can proceed because detailed information is available.

Over time, an experienced fraud examiner will notice that similarities often exist when comparing the details of various fraud scenarios. Although this is certainly not an absolute, the vast majority of embezzlement schemes share the following:

➤ Weak internal controls
➤ Too much trust
➤ Poor management oversight
➤ Lack of a financial audit
➤ No background checks on key positions
➤ Lack of independent checks on bank statements and credit card statements
➤ Failure to take advantage of the bank's Positive Pay service
➤ Failure to take advantage of the bank's Lockbox service

Another striking consistency that has surfaced over time is *when* most of the embezzlements addressed in this book occurred, and this is *between the time the auditors conclude their field work for one year and return to start their field work for the subsequent year.* Obviously, the perpetrators of a scam, regardless of how clever, will in all likelihood put the fraudulent activity on hold while the auditors are physically in the office, as they want to give the impression to the auditors that they are squeaky clean. In other words, while the auditors are on-site, there will be no ghosts on the payroll, there will be no check tampering or switching, there will be no ghost vendors, and so on.

Something to Consider

Consider having the independent CPA pay a surprise visit to the client's offices on a day while the window is open, that being of course a business day during the window of opportunity for embezzlement.

The Surprise Visit

The auditors will select a day for the surprise visit at their discretion. For this surprise visit to be effective, consider the following:

1. With management's permission, of course, the auditors should have the client's bank send a cut-off bank statement directly to their offices, *not* to the client's office. This statement should include copies of the front and back of checks.

2. Have the client's credit card company send a cut-off statement to the accountant's office, as with the bank statement.

3. Transaction tests:

Purchases

Prior to the surprise visit, the accounting firm should send unknown "shoppers" to the establishment, as follows:

Cash: One of the shoppers should purchase items for cash and check to see that the items were rung up properly on the cash register and that a receipt was issued for the purchase.

Check: One of the shoppers should make a purchase with a personal check and observe that procedures were followed.

Credit: One of the shoppers should use a credit card and monitor credit card procedures.

Mail: If the client sells goods or services via the mail, test the system by carefully monitoring purchases made by credit card, check, and even cash.

Internet: If the client sells goods or services via a website, make test purchases as noted above.

4. On-site work relating to purchases:

   A. Trace the cash purchases to ensure that these transactions were not voided *after* the shopper left the premises. Obviously, if they were, a serious problem exists.

   B. Trace the credit card purchases to the cut-off credit card statement to ensure that the proper amount was recorded to the proper card.

   C. Thoroughly audit the check transactions by carefully examining the checks or check images. In particular, compare the test check endorsement stamps and bank clearinghouse stamps with other checks to ensure they that match and that someone hasn't opened up an account at another bank under the same or similar name as the client's business name.

5. Other on-site work:

   Payroll: Thoroughly investigate new employees hired after field work was concluded, to ensure that there are no ghosts on the payroll (See "Ghosts on the Payroll and Ghost Vendors" in Section 4 of this manual).

Payroll taxes: Audit the accuracy of the payroll tax liability and actual tax deposits for federal, state, and local payroll taxes to ensure that there have been no intentional tax overpayments credited to any individual income tax withholding account.

New vendors: Organizations should have an approved and updated vendor listing examined by the auditors during field work. New vendors added to this list should be investigated by the auditors to ensure that they actually exist and that there are no ghost vendors (See "Ghosts on the Payroll and Ghost Vendors" in Section 4 of this manual).

Tip: Examine new vendor invoices carefully. Pay close attention to and investigate new vendors that show only a post office box remittance address and no street address. Not indicating a street address on an invoice is unusual and should be investigated.

Bank reconciliations, current year: Select a random bank reconciliation prepared internally by staff and check it carefully as follows:

a. Ensure that all checks have been accounted for, and investigate any missing checks.

b. Investigate any new or unusual bank debit memoranda. A common "window of opportunity" trick is to have insurance payments, car payments, and the like paid for by debit memoranda drawn against the checking account during this period, and canceling these prior to the auditors arriving to start field work.

c. Investigate any out-of-sequence checks.

d. Test deposits.

Bank reconciliations, last month of the prior year: Here is another common scam:

Someone approves a legitimate invoice for payment early in the last month of the fiscal year and forwards the approved invoice to finance for payment. An accountant prepares the check, has it signed, and mails it to the vendor, who cashes the check accordingly. This check or check image will be in the end of the month bank statement.

Unknown to anyone, the dishonest accountant intentionally prepares a second check payable to the same vendor for the same amount of money and for the same invoice, in another check run, but places this check in the office safe. Typically, the fraudulent check will be made payable to a very clever variation of the legitimate vendor's name. For example, if the legitimate vendor is the Acme Printing *Corp.*, the second check may be made out to the Acme Printing *Co.*, and the possibility of discovering this would be very remote.

The auditors start their field work and the accountant crosses his or her fingers, hoping the auditors do not catch the double payment.

If the auditors *do* discover the double payment, typically they would bring it to the staff accountant's attention, and he would probably feign embarrassment over the double payment error, but would be able to produce the check for the second payment (it is still in the office safe), show it to the auditors, simply void the check, and correct the transaction by an adjusting journal entry.

At this point nothing looks suspicious to the auditors, because mistakes can happen, particularly at the end of the year when the accounting staff is busy with budgets, taxes, W-2 preparation, and so forth.

But what if the auditors *don't* discover the double payment, which is also possible? Simple—the perpetrator waits for field work to be concluded (the window of opportunity just opened), opens a bank account in the name of the payee of the fraudulent check, deposit the second check, waits for the funds to become available, closes the account out at that time, and pockets the money!

What is the possibility that the auditors will discover this? Very low, *because this transaction occurred on the prior year's records, which have already been audited!*

Tip: During the course of the surprise visit, revisit the end of the prior year's bank reconciliation and track the status of checks outstanding on that statement. In particular, compare the endorsement stamps appearing on these checks against other checks deposited by the same vendor, and ensure that they match.

Inventory: The surprise visit is an opportune time to examine inventory rather than waiting for field work to commence.

Tip: Open up and examine the contents of boxes of *inexpensive* inventory, particularly if there are any marks on the box. A common trick is for an employee to put an *expensive* item in a box for an inexpensive item when no one is looking and carefully place and mark the box. An accomplice could easily enter the establishment, pick up the marked box, and present it to a cashier for payment. The cashier would scan the bar code, charge the lesser amount, and watch the accomplice walk out of the store.

Tip: Assuming the client's type of inventory qualifies, of course, consider recommending that the client purchase a clear-plastic, shrink-wrap machine. If possible, wrap incoming inventory boxes in this clear plastic and safeguard the machine. Simply wrapping boxes in clear plastic greatly reduces the possibility of switching expensive and inexpensive items.

Statement of Auditing Standard No. 99 "Consideration of Fraud in a Financial Statement Audit"

Statement of Auditing Standard No. 99 "Consideration of Fraud in a Financial Statement Audit"

AN AUDIT BY an independent CPA firm is not designed to uncover fraudulent activity. The purpose of an audit is to provide reasonable assurance that the financial statements do not include any material misstatement as a result of fraudulent activity. During the auditing process, the CPA firm may uncover fraud, but this is not the reason the auditors are there.

In response to well-publicized incidents implicating auditors, the accounting profession promulgated **Statement of Auditing Standard No. 99,** "Consideration of Fraud in a Financial Statement Audit."

The primary objectives of this new auditing standard are the following:

1. Renew the public's confidence in audit quality.

2. Detect misleading financial statements.

Although the auditing CPA is still not held *responsible* or accountable for failing to detect fraud, the new standard does impose several new responsibilities on auditing CPAs in the areas of:

1. Understanding the key elements of the Fraud Triangle

2. Improved audit planning by requiring brainstorming sessions among audit team members

3. Requiring a better understanding of the client's business

4. Inquiries of key client personnel relating to existing or potential lapses in internal controls that may lead to fraud

5. Analytical procedures based on professional skepticism

6. Documentation of information gathering

The Fraud Triangle

The *cornerstone* of SAS 99 is to educate both auditors and management about the conditions that are usually present when fraud occurs, and this is best understood by taking into consideration the three corners of the Fraud Triangle, as described in Section 1:

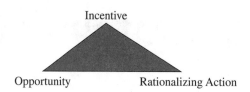

Incentive: There are endless incentives to commit a dishonest act, including financial hardship; vices such as drugs, alcohol, or gambling; employee grievances; and the desire for material goods, among others. Desperate people often take desperate action.

Opportunity: The primary opportunity to commit fraud is provided by poor or weak internal controls. An incentive to steal coupled with an opportunity in the form of poor internal controls is a dangerous combination.

Rationalizing Action: Obviously, some fraudulent acts are committed by people fully aware that they are perpetrating a crime, and their conscience produces no guilt. However, others feel they are righting a perceived wrong, such as a salary inequity, and have convinced themselves that they have earned and are owed the financial results of fraudulent acts, and therefore they are not stealing.

Once the auditing CPA understands that the elements of the Fraud Triangle are present in virtually all fraud, he or she is ready to proceed with the technical requirements of the new standard.

Improved Audit Planning

SAS 99 requires the audit team to improve the quality of the audit by mandating documented brainstorming sessions among audit personnel to assess client fraud risk.

Tip: Although it will not seem natural, the audit team members should strive to "think like a thief thinks!" during this session. With this in mind, a sample of questions that may be included in the audit team brainstorming session are:

➤ Are there any procedures that you are not comfortable with?

➤ What existing weaknesses in internal controls could be exploited?

➤ Who or what staff positions may be capable of perpetuating an embezzlement?

➤ How could revenues be misappropriated?

➤ Is collusion among staff a possibility?

➤ Is collusion among staff and customers or vendors a possibility?

➤ Which client employees should be interviewed?

➤ Has the client experienced fraud in the past, and how did the perpetrator do it?

Tip: The most effective way to conduct a brainstorming session among audit team members is to appoint a session facilitator, usually one of the senior staff. The role of the facilitator is to ensure that the golden rule of brainstorming is followed: **There are no dumb questions, observations, or suggestions, and criticism is forbidden!**

Also, remember to summarize and *document* the brainstorming session to supplement audit work papers.

Understanding the Client's Business

SAS 99 requires auditors to improve their understanding of the client's business, to better assess fraud risk. Basic building blocks to educate the auditor about the client's business include:

1. Comparison of actual versus budget revenues and expenses and investigation of material variances

2. Compilation of a five-year actual revenue and expense trend analysis and investigation of material variances

3. Utilizing outside resources—for example, comparing the client's financial statements to the financial statements of similar clients and investigating material variances

Tip: An often overlooked but excellent resource to help the auditor to better understand the client's business is the local or national association that represents your client's profession. The saying "there's an association for everything" is probably true, and very often these associations compile and sell operating ratio reports. These reports gather information, typically by budget size, for their members' balance sheets, revenues, and expenses. Compare client financials to average financials of the same budget size, and investigate material variances. These reports are excellent resources to supplement audit planning with regard to assessing risk. Finally, these reports and studies are documented audit plan proof that the CPA has taken the initiative to truly understand the nature of the client's business.

Inquiries of Client Personnel

An aspect of the Sarbanes-Oxley Act that affects SAS 99 is mandatory inquiries of certain client personnel. Some fraudulent acts would have been exposed if only people were asked if they knew of the existence of fraud. Some people won't come forth and volunteer information unless they are asked, because they are shy, reluctant to get involved, or the like.

Who should be interviewed?

The decision as to who should be asked fraud inquiry questions is made by the audit team, typically during the brainstorming session. Positions to consider include, but are not limited to:

➤ The chief executive officer
➤ The treasurer
➤ The chief financial officer
➤ The controller
➤ Accounts payable clerks
➤ Accounts receivable clerks
➤ Those handling checks or cash
➤ Security personnel
➤ Personnel who order inventory
➤ Personnel responsible for safeguarding inventory, such as warehouse personnel

And don't forget:

➤ The human resources manager (this person *always* knows what's going on!)

What questions should be asked?

The decision about what questions to ask is also a result of the brainstorming session, and is up to the judgment of the audit team.

Tip: Before making inquiries, put employees at ease and gain their confidence by telling them that auditors are *required* and have a duty to ask these questions, and that they have not been selected due to any suspicions of dishonesty.

Typical questions may include:

➤ Are you aware of the existence of fraud?
➤ Have you ever been offered expensive gifts or cash by anyone attempting to conduct business with the organization?
➤ Are you aware of any potential for fraud?
➤ Has anyone ever approached you to be an accomplice in a fraud scheme?
➤ Do you know what to do if you become aware of or are suspicious of illegal or unethical acts?
➤ Are you aware of any conflicts of interest either within or outside of the organization that could lead to collusion or increased fraud risk?

Tip: Although the Sarbanes-Oxley Act mandates whistleblower protection for public companies, it currently does not apply to nonpublic businesses or nonprofit organizations.

Depending upon the nature of the client, of course consider recommending that the client adopt a mechanism to report suspected fraud and a whistleblower policy prohibiting retaliation. Clients typically appreciate this recommendation, and documenting the suggestion in audit work papers attests that the auditors have taken seriously their responsibility to improve internal controls and assist their client in exposing fraud and reducing fraud risk. (See "Whistleblowers," in Section 3 of this handbook.)

CASE STUDY: QUITE A TRIP!

When analyzing the new client's business, the brainstorming team became aware that the client outsourced the accounting function to an accounting service. The accounting service had their client representative visit the client one day a week to pick up information, have discussions, and so forth.

The brainstorming team decided to interview this person, even though this accounting representative was not even on the client staff.

One of the questions posed to this person was, "Do any of the existing procedures make you uncomfortable?"

The accounting representative answered, "Yes, I've never been comfortable with the way they handle their company credit card transactions."

The resulting conversations and actions are very interesting:

"What makes you uncomfortable?"

"I've never seen the credit card detail. The CEO gives me a copy of the remittance advice and some codes to post to, but I've never seen the credit card detail itself."

"Where do they keep the credit card statements?"

"It's my understanding the CEO has the credit card bill sent to him personally to his home."

Based on this answer, the audit team made the decision to investigate credit card transactions very carefully. After securing the appropriate approvals, they had the credit card company forward copies of credit card statements for the prior six months directly to their offices. Their review of the statements led to uncovering a very clever and interesting embezzlement.

The audit team discovered that the CEO had been charging several thousand dollars a month to a national restaurant chain's local establishment. Through further inquiries, they later learned that the CEO's girlfriend was the assistant manager of the restaurant. Armed with this information, they contacted the internal audit department at the national restaurant's headquarters, told them something suspicious was taking place, gave them the parties' names, and asked for their cooperation in investigating the situation. A few weeks later, a representative of the national restaurant chain contacted the auditors and informed them of what they had found: It seems that when the CEO had dinner at the local restaurant, his girlfriend, the assistant manager, always waited on him personally. What he would do was give her a tip of $1,000 or more for a single dinner! Because she was in the right position as assistant manager, she simply manipulated the records for the day such that the excessive tip was directed to her personally.

All of this was discovered directly because of good interview questions and follow-up!

Analytical Procedures/Professional Skepticism

SAS 99 requires the use of analytical procedures to identify misleading financial statements that indicate fraud, basically requiring auditors to maintain a questioning mind.

As stated earlier, an excellent resource is an operating ratio report compiled by the association representing your client's profession. Compare your client's financials to national averages for the same budget bracket, and investigate significant variances.

Other analytical procedures may include:

➤ Gather a few years of *internal* monthly financial statements, and compare the same months over the different years to see if anything appears unusual.

➤ Track revenue and expense trend ratios from year to year, and investigate unusual blips.

Tip: Don't rule out that management may have *intentionally* misstated financials in order to qualify for loans, lines of credit, or the like. Embezzlement may not be present or an incentive in this case.

If Fraud Is Detected

In the event that fraud is detected within the organization, the CPA generally is not required to advise outside authorities. This is not the auditors' responsibility, unless there are some legal requirements to do so. They are, however, required to bring any issue they uncover to the appropriate level of management for resolution.

Other Areas an Auditing CPA Might Investigate

In addition to those detailed in this book, the auditing CPA will probably assess several other areas of exposure to fraud and manipulation of financial statements. These include, but are not limited to, the following schemes:

Cash Theft Schemes

➤ Cash skimming
➤ Sales skimming

- Unrecorded sales
- Sales during nonbusiness hours
- Theft of checks
- Check tampering
- Forged endorsements
- Cash register schemes
- Fraudulent bank reconciliations
- Deposit lapping
- Altered payees
- Converting stolen checks
- Altering receipts
- Fabricating sales records
- Altering cash counts
- Altering deposits
- False accounts
- Voided transactions

Billing Schemes

- Setting up "shell companies"
- Fraudulent invoicing
- Collusion with vendors
- Pass-through schemes
- Overbilling
- Kickbacks
- Diverting business for personal use
- Pay-and-return schemes
- False purchase orders
- Returning merchandise for cash

Accounts Receivable Schemes

- Lapping
- False credits
- False discounts
- Unauthorized write-offs
- Collection agency schemes
- Unauthorized credit card refunds
- Collusion with customers
- Skimming
- Forcing balances

➤ Debiting fictitious accounts

➤ Stolen statements

Inventory Schemes

➤ Theft and subsequent sale

➤ Over/understating on financial statements

➤ Sales returns

➤ Concealment

➤ Purchasing schemes

➤ Kickbacks

➤ Fictional vendors

➤ Padding inventory records

➤ Concealing shrinkages

➤ Falsified receiving reports

➤ Shifts between locations

➤ Diversion of inventory

➤ Short and false shipments

Fixed Asset Schemes

➤ Theft

➤ Conversion for personal use

➤ Manipulation and concealment

➤ Improper capitalization of expenses

Accounts Payable Schemes

➤ Kickbacks

➤ False or inflated vendor invoices

➤ Improper purchasing

➤ Duplicate payment schemes

➤ Theft or misappropriation of payments

➤ Contract or bidding fraud

➤ Ghost vendors

Payroll Schemes

➤ Ghosts on the payroll

➤ Commission schemes

➤ False Workers' Compensation claims

➤ Diversion of tax payments

➤ Overpayments, false wages, false pay rates

- Diverting wages
- Keeping former employees on payroll

Computer Schemes

- Entering false transactions
- Bogus file maintenance transactions
- Failure to enter data
- Altering data
- Manipulation of accounts

Fictitious Financial Reporting Schemes

- Understated liabilities
- Recording fictitious assets
- Improper capitalization of expenses
- Sham transactions
- Improper revenue recognition
- Overstated accounts receivables
- Overly complex transactions

Debt/Equity Schemes

- Unauthorized borrowing
- Division of loan proceeds
- Stock and dividend manipulation

Expense Account Schemes

- Overstated reimbursement requests
- Altered supporting documentation
- Fictitious receipts
- Multiple reimbursements
- Claiming expenses paid by others
- Substituting expensive air fare itineraries for those of discount carriers

Other Important Areas of Concern

- Asset flipping
- Credit card exposures
- Conflicts of interest
- Employee lifestyles

SECTION 3

Essential Internal Control and Administrative Procedures to Avoid Embezzlement

The Background Check

IN OUR LITIGIOUS society, it is becoming increasingly difficult to get honest references from previous employers for new employee candidates. In fact, when a company contacts a prospective employee's prior employer, the organization will typically only provide verification of the person's title and the duration of the employee's term of employment.

This makes hiring very difficult today. It means that, in the hiring process, employers have to rely almost exclusively on the accuracy of the individual's application or résumé, plus the honesty of the individual during the interview stage. Ultimately, you can assume that this means you will know virtually nothing about your new hires.

The only sure way to find out what you need to know about the prospect is to request permission to perform a background check. While you wouldn't expect, or impose, a background check for every position within your organization, you should consider it for key positions, particularly those in finance and those that involve handling checks, credit cards, and cash.

You must ask the potential employee for permission to conduct a background check, and that permission should be in writing. Of course, prospective employees have the right to deny permission and, legally, this is not supposed to be taken into consideration during the hiring process. If you have any doubt at all, check with your attorney.

It is critically important to receive permission from prospective employees (always check with your attorney first for guidance) to conduct a thorough background check for the following positions:

➤ *All* employees in accounting and finance
➤ Other employees handling cash, checks, or credit cards
➤ The human resources manager
➤ Other positions that management feels are key

There are services such as private investigative firms whose business it is to conduct these background checks; this fee is very affordable and offsets the possible risk of hiring the wrong person.

At a minimum, a background check should include the following:

1. **Criminal Background Check**

   If an individual has been convicted of a crime, the matter is public record. Obviously, a check of criminal activity is vital with regard to the positions named.

   Criminal background checks should be conducted at the following:

   ➤ The state of residence
   ➤ The state of employment
   ➤ The states adjacent to the states of residence or employment
   ➤ Other states noted on the prospect's application, such as prior employment states, and the like

2. **Credit Check**

   Credit checks are very easy to obtain, and the three primary credit agencies are:

   ➤ Experian
   ➤ Equifax
   ➤ TransUnion

   Any problem with credit history is a cause for alarm, but obviously people with *serious* credit problems could become desperate and should *never* be hired for key positions.

3. **References**

   A check on references is important, but realistically, no one would include a bad reference on an application. Compounding this is the fact that most employers are only going to release information such as the person's title and length of employment, due to fear of litigation.

Tip: As stated, no one is going to list a poor reference on a résumé, but any significant time periods *between* jobs may indicate a problem at an unnamed employer.

4. **Social Security Number**

   A verification of an applicant's Social Security number is important, because it is common for someone to be hired under a fictitious number or someone else's Social Security number.

   Why?

   A common ruse is to be hired using someone else's Social Security number and file a W-4 with several dependents, resulting in little or no federal and state income taxes being withheld. At the same time, this person could be collecting unemployment, food stamps, and other subsidies from the state. Important: It is now possible to verify Social Security numbers directly via the Social Security Administration. However, this verification is offered only *after* someone is hired.

5. **Driving Record**

   Surprisingly, it is important to check driving records through the Department of Motor Vehicles.

   Why?

   A poor driving record would not preclude hiring someone, but *don't* have the person run errands and the like for the organization. If this person unfortunately gets into an accident during the course of the work day, while doing business for the organization, you can count on the business itself to be named in any resulting legal action.

6. **Education and Degrees Attained**

   Community colleges, colleges, and universities will verify academic credentials as well as grade transcripts. The education verification will expose any embellished educational background.

7. **Professional Credentials**

   If the employee candidate has professional credentials such as attorney, CPA, industry certifications, and so forth, these credentials are easily checked. Ensure that the individual actually has these credentials and that licenses are current.

   Additionally, it may be wise to include the following:

8. **Drug Testing**

9. **FBI Fingerprint Check**

Remember that you have to get the prospective employee's permission to conduct a background check. Also, be certain to have a knowledgeable labor law attorney review a draft of the permission form before implementing the form, to ensure it meets federal and state laws.

A *draft* of a Permission to Conduct a Background Check may appear as follows:

Permission to Conduct
Background Checks

I ___(employee name)___ do hereby give permission to conduct a background check both before and anytime subsequent to employment.

I understand this background check may include the following areas:

- Criminal
- Credit
- References
- Social Security Number
- Driving Record
- Education and Degrees Attained
- Professional Credentials
- Drug Testing
- FBI Fingerprint Check

I also acknowledge and understand that if any information included on my Application for Employment, Résumé, Curriculum Vitae or any other document related to my employment is later found to be false, my employment may be terminated immediately for cause.

Employee Signature _____

Date _____

Witness Name _____

Witness Signature _____

Date _____

Conditions of Employment Agreement

The necessity for thorough background checks was covered earlier in this section. The Conditions of Employment agreement is another important employment document that employees should sign before hire.

The most important elements to be included in this document are:

1. **Termination for Erroneous Statements**

   A potential employee's application and résumé will typically include education information, prior employment positions, professional credentials, references, and other important information. Additionally, the application form should inquire if the applicant has ever been convicted of a felony. Once the employee signs the application, that person attests that the information is truthful.

   Part of the Conditions of Employment document should clearly state that the organization has reserved the right of termination of employment if any of this information is later proven false.

2. **Offers and Acceptance of Gifts**

   It is common for an unscrupulous vendor to unethically or sometimes even illegally try to influence employees by offering them gifts. Obviously, trivial gift offers such as candy during the holidays is no cause for concern, but offers of expensive gifts and cash constitute bribes, and it is important to include in the Conditions of Employment agreement that such gift offers must be reported to management.

3. **Management Day**

   The Conditions of Employment agreement should state that management has reserved the right to direct an employee not to report to work on a day at *management's* discretion (with pay). The employee acknowledges that management has reserved the right to have another employee assume his or her responsibilities on this day, sit at his or her desk and review mail, and the like.

   Additionally, a management representative (with a witness) has reserved the right to inspect the contents of the employee's desk, review websites the employee visits, review emails, and so on.

4. **Uninterrupted Vacation**

   The Conditions of Employment agreement should state that management has reserved the right to *require* employees to take at least one full week of vacation per year.

   Additionally, as noted in item 3 above, during this week management may have another employee sit at the absent employee's desk, inspect desk contents, turn on the computer, and so forth.

5. **Sick Days**

The Conditions of Employment agreement should also note that the same actions that management may take on the Management Day and during Uninterrupted Vacation also apply to sick days.

6. **Involuntary Terminations/Leaves of Absence**

The Conditions of Employment agreement should state clearly the following:

> ➤ Discussions regarding involuntary terminations and leaves of absence will *not* take place in the employee's office, cubicle, or similar location. Rather, the discussion will be held in an office of the management team or a neutral location such as a conference room, library, or the like. Remember that the offender's office probably contains important evidence that the offender should not have access to.

> ➤ At a minimum, termination discussions should *always* include a witness selected by management to verify exactly what was said during the discussion, and the manager and witness should prepare notes immediately after the discussion and record important statements, actions, and so on. Additionally, reserve the right to have other parties attend, if deemed necessary, such as a lawyer, CPA, police officer, or the like.
>
> If a man has to confront a woman, the witness should be another woman. If a woman finds it necessary to confront a man, the witness should be another man. This, of course, lessens the chance of being accused of any sexual impropriety.

7. **Surrender of Organization Intellectual Property**

Work produced by an employee during the course of employment, such as correspondence, reports, studies, books, or articles, is considered intellectual property and *is the property of the organization.* This fact should be communicated to the prospective employee to avoid any misunderstandings at termination.

8. **Surrender of Customer Information**

Many employees have access to sensitive customer information such as credit card numbers, checking account numbers, Social Security numbers, addresses, telephone numbers, and the like. The Conditions of Employment agreement should state that this information may not be removed from the office under any circumstances, but particularly at termination of employment.

9. **Immediate Removal from Office**

The Conditions of Employment agreement should be clear in stating that, immediately upon termination:

> ➤ The employee will surrender such items as door keys, credit cards, and the like.

➤ The employee will not be allowed to return to his or her office, cubicle, or other work area. If the employee needs essential personal items such as a purse, wallet, car keys, *two* other employees will retrieve them for the employee (requiring two other employees to retrieve these items eliminates accusations such as theft).

➤ The employee will then be escorted directly out of the building.

➤ Other personal effects (photos, pictures, etc.) will be gathered by *two* other employees, and these items will be later delivered to the employee's residence via courier.

10. **Prosecution**

The document should state very clearly that in the event an embezzlement or fraud is proven, the organization *will prosecute* the offending employee, regardless of the dollar amount involved, to the full extent of the law.

This threat of prosecution is an effective deterrent against fraud. If the employee has any questions concerning prosecution, explain that a prosecution may result in a criminal record, and this would obviously affect future employment at other organizations.

A Conditions of Employment agreement document may appear as follows:

Conditions of Employment Agreement Form

I, ___(employee name)___, an employee of ___(organization)___ acknowledge and agree to the following Conditions of Employment:

1. Termination for Erroneous Statements

I understand that if any information provided by me and noted on my original APPLICATION FOR EMPLOYMENT or related documents provided by me such as a RÉSUMÉ or CURRICULUM VITAE is later proven to be false, these misstatements are grounds for termination of employment.

These misstatements include, but are not limited to, education, professional credentials, prior employers, prior positions, job responsibilities, references, arrest record, etc.

2. Offers of Gifts by Vendors

I understand that acceptance of offers of expensive gifts or cash by vendors will be considered acceptance of a bribe and may be cause for disciplinary action or termination of employment.

I also understand that I have a responsibility to report such offers to the appropriate level of management.

3. Management Day

I understand that management has reserved the right to direct me not to report to work on a day of management's discretion (with pay).

I also understand that management has reserved the right to direct another employee to assume my responsibilities, sit at my desk, review mail, etc.

I further understand that a management representative and a witness may inspect the contents of my desk, review my computer files including websites I have been visiting, email messages, etc.

I agree to abide by the provisions of the EMPLOYEE HANDBOOK and if unallowable items such as alcohol, illegal drugs, pornography, etc. are discovered, this will be grounds for immediate termination of employment for cause.

4. Uninterrupted Vacation

I understand that I am required to take at least one full week of uninterrupted vacation per year and that management may mandate this vacation if I fail to schedule it voluntarily.

On this time off, I also understand that management has reserved the right to have another employee assume my responsibilities, inspect the contents of my desk as well as other action noted in Item 3 above.

5. Sick Days

I understand that the actions management has reserved the right to take in Items 3 and 4 noted in this document also apply to any sick days I may take.

6. Involuntary Terminations/Leaves of Absence

I understand that discussions concerning my involuntary termination or leave of absence will take place at a location other than my office, cubicle, etc. such as an office of management, conference room, library, etc.

I also understand that this discussion will include a witness and management has reserved the right to also include attorneys, CPAs, police officers, etc. at their discretion.

7. Surrender of Organization Intellectual Property

I understand that all work products that I produce during my employment, as well as works-in-progress, are the organization's intellectual property. Upon my termination, whether voluntary or involuntary, this property and supporting documents will not be removed from the office under any circumstances, and I may not use this information for any purpose without the express written permission of management.

This property includes, but is not limited to:

➢ Correspondence
➢ Reports
➢ Studies
➢ Books
➢ Articles
➢ Accounting Records
➢ Videos

8. Surrender of Customer/Employee Information

I understand that I may come into contact with sensitive information regarding customers and employees, and in this respect I agree to keep this information confidential and I understand this information may not leave the office for any reason.

This information includes, but is not limited to:

➢ Credit card information
➢ Bank account information
➢ Social Security numbers
➢ Telephone numbers
➢ Addresses
➢ Mailing lists
➢ Prospect lists

9. Immediate Removal from Office

I understand and agree to the following in the event of my involuntary termination or leave of absence:

➢ I will surrender such items as organization door keys, credit cards, etc. at management's request.
➢ I will be escorted directly out of the office and will not be allowed to return to my personal office, cubicle, etc.
➢ In the event I require essential personal items such as a purse, wallet, car keys, etc., two employees will recover these items from my office for me.
➢ Nonessential personal effects such as photographs, etc. will be gathered by two employees and these items will be delivered to my residence via courier.

10. Prosecution

I understand that if fraud or embezzlement are proven, management may proceed with prosecution to the full extent of the law, regardless of the dollar amount of the incident.

I also understand that prosecution may result in a criminal record that may affect my prospects for future employment elsewhere.

11. Background Check

I understand that, in accordance with the *Permissions to Conduct Background Checks Form*, the organization has reserved the right to conduct background checks anytime subsequent to my unemployment.

I hereby state that I have read and understand this Conditions of Employment agreement and the Employee Handbook and agree to abide by the conditions therein.

Employee Name _____

Employee Signature _____

Date _____

Management Representative Name _____

Management Representative Signature _____

Date _____

Note: This material is not intended as legal advice. Before implementing these suggestions, be certain to have them reviewed by a competent employment law attorney familiar with your state and federal employment laws.

Tip: When the employee signs and dates the agreement, have Human Resources make a copy of it and place the *copy* in the employee's personnel file. Place the original in a location to which the employee has no access, such as a safe deposit box or safe.

As stated elsewhere in this handbook, it is very important to protect the original document, because it may be evidence in the event of a criminal proceeding. In the event of an incident, if the offending employee removed this document, it could weaken a criminal case because a defense attorney could assert that the employee was never made aware of the ramifications of his or her actions and would not have proceeded with the fraud if he or she had known it would result in dire consequences.

CASE STUDY: THE VALUE OF IMPLEMENTING THE MANAGEMENT DAY POLICY:

A CEO owned a small chain of automobile repair shops, and each shop was run by a general manager. The general managers were eligible for a sizable year-end bonus based on the net profit of the store for the year.

Unknown to the CEO, one of the general managers concocted a scheme to inflate the store's net profit and hence increase his bonus. What he would do was convince an unknowing customer that an expensive part was needed to repair his car. The customer, assuming that the general manager was honest, agreed to the repair and paid the bill when it was presented. The invoice included a bill for the expensive part and labor, but the part was never installed. This scheme significantly increased the store's net profit, of course, because it billed for parts with no cost, and labor that was not actually provided.

The CEO decided to implement the Management Day policy and directed the offending general manager to take a day off with pay. The general manager was prohibited from coming to the shop this day and his responsibilities were assumed by the assistant manager.

On this day off, one of the unknowingly bilked customers came to the shop complaining he still had problems with his car. He presented his receipt to the assistant manager, who discovered that the expensive part was never installed, exposing the scam.

Conflicts of Interest

It is inevitable that conflicts of interest will arise in an organization. This can occur on all levels, whether the board of directors or staff.

Therefore, everyone who works for, or represents, the organization (including board members, staff, committee members, and so forth) must sign a Conflict of Interest form.

This serves to raise the level of awareness that the organization does not tolerate or defend conflicts of interest. Additionally, this will encourage reporting of all real or perceived conflicts of interest. For the protection of everyone involved, these conflicts should be brought to the attention of the level of authority necessary for consideration, resolution, and direction.

Conflict of Interest Form

I have been informed of this organization's policy regarding conflicts of interest. I agree to bring to the attention of the proper level of authority any real, or perceived, conflicts of interest that may arise during the course of my tenure with this organization.

Such conflicts include, but are not limited to, personal or professional affiliations, relationships with family and friends, dealings with other organizations or businesses, political considerations, or relationships with other boards of directors.

Additionally, I agree to abide by the direction and decision of management. I understand that failure to advise management of such conflicts may result in disciplinary action, termination of employment, or removal from my position.

Name _____

Position_____

Signature _____

Date _____

Nepotism

Employing relatives is usually a very bad idea. Initially, it may seem to be a quick solution to a hiring issue, but it may very well backfire. Over and above the normal day-to-day tensions that can happen in the workplace, collusion is much more likely to occur among family members than among unrelated employees.

To protect your company, you probably should have a nepotism policy across the board. If that is not feasible, or desirable, you should consider, at the very least, a modified, department-specific policy. This will effectively prevent and prohibit the employment of family members in any area where you feel most vulnerable and, in particular, the accounting function.

The policy should also state that family members will not be hired for, or transferred into, positions where they will have direct or indirect supervision of one another.

This will save you a lot of headaches and human resources problems in the future.

As with all forms and policies suggested in this manual, review the Nepotism Policy and Nepotism form with a competent attorney.

Sample Nepotism Policy

It is the policy of the company that no employee shall be employed in a position in which the employee must report directly or indirectly to a family member (immediate or extended family), spouse, partner, significant other, or someone with whom the employee lives.

If two employees should become spouses, partners, significant others, or choose to live together, one must resign if one reports directly or indirectly to the other. Failure to voluntarily resign will result in the involuntary termination of one of the parties at the discretion of management.

Employee Name _____

Employee Signature _____

Date _____